Student
YOUTH COURT
Training Manual

Student Youth Court Training Manual

1ST EDITION, FEBRUARY 2020

educational and juvenile justice reform

Tessa Hannigan
Nya Kuziwa
Gregg Volz, Esq.

Arch Street Press
Bryn Mawr, PA • USA

First Arch Street Press edition February 2020

ARCH STREET PRESS, ARCH ST. PRESS
and colophon are registered trademarks of Arch Street Press.

For information about special discounts for bulk purchases, please contact Arch Street Press: sales@archstreetpress.org.

Cover jacket and book design by idesign communications

Library of Congress Cataloging-in-Publication Data is available.

ISBN: 978-1-938798-29-0

I want to thank Tessa Hannigan and Nya Kuziwa for their assistance in the summer of 2019 to help develop this training manual for use by youth court students. I also want to thank the Lang Center at Swarthmore College for providing internships to both of them—allowing them to work on this manual.

CONTENTS

CHAPTER 1
INTRODUCTION TO YOUTH COURT

Can you think of a time when you didn't do the right thing? Maybe you took something without asking, or you said something mean that hurt your friend's feelings? How did you feel when that happened, and what did you do to make things right? Taking responsibility for hurtful behavior is one of the hardest things we can do, and sometimes it's hard to know where to begin.

When we do things that negatively impact other people's lives or that inflict pain, we have caused harm, which can be physical, mental, emotional, social, economic or any combination of these. When someone causes harm, he or she has an obligation to remedy it. The goal of Youth Court is to help students take responsibility for their actions when they have caused harm, to help them understand what the harm was, and to think of ways to repair that harm. To reach this goal, Youth Court members (that's you!) work as a team to answer three guiding questions:

1. What harm was caused and by whom?
2. What were the root causes of the harm?
3. What needs to happen in order to repair this harm and prevent future harm?

Activities

1.1 Brainstorm

- What is harm? What do you think needs to happen when a classmate causes harm?
- If you were in charge of your school, what would you do when students misbehave?

1.2 Reflection

- What are some ideas or feelings you had in this lesson?
- What do Youth Courts do?
- Have you or a friend gotten in trouble in school before? What happened? Do you think you were treated fairly?
- Many adults think that punishment is the best deterrent against bad behavior. Do you agree?

CHAPTER 2
RULES AND FAIRNESS

In Chapter 1, we discussed consequences of harmful behavior. In this chapter we look at rules. Why do we have them? How do they set boundaries on our behavior? What happens if we break them?

There are natural consequences to everything we do. For example, if you sleep through your alarm, the natural consequence is that you'll be late for school. Or if you bully someone, the natural consequence is that a person has been emotionally hurt. When our actions violate a rule created by our school or government (like your school's rules against bullying), then additional consequences are often imposed. The usual consequence for breaking a rule is punishment—but it does not have to be.

Rules exist to maintain safety and fairness for everybody, so the consequences for breaking those rules should also be fair and restorative. In Youth Courts, we have the opportunity to understand how behavior can cause harm and create a consequence that is helpful and healing, instead of punitive (punishment). Let's examine the purpose of rules together! Are they always fair? Can we rely on rules to create justice?

Activities

2.1 Brainstorm

- Think of a school rule: How and to whom is it helpful? Or, if you think the rule is harmful, how and to whom is it harmful?
- Should students have a voice in school rules?

2.2 Why do we have rules?

Sample Case #1:
School policy forbids cheating on tests. Alicia is caught cheating on a test and is written up. It turns out that her parents decided if she does not get an A on this test, they would punish her. Alicia is scared she is not smart enough to get an A without cheating, so she cheated.

Sample Case #2:
School policy also forbids carrying weapons. Kahlaa carries a pocket knife because she knows that several assaults have recently occurred in her neighborhood. One day her pocket knife fell out in the classroom. The teacher confiscated the knife and wrote her up for possessing a weapon.

Sample Case #3:
Maria's school has a strict dress code: Students must wear blue-, black- or white-collared tops, and khaki or navy bottoms. Maria owns only three shirts that fit the dress code and can't afford to buy more right now. One day, Maria wears a dark-brown shirt and gets in trouble for a dress-code violation. Her other clothes were dirty that day and she lives in an apartment building, so her family has to pay for laundry. Her mother gets her paycheck on Fridays, so she was waiting until the weekend to do the laundry.

1. Why does school policy prohibit these things and enforce these rules? Do those reasons make sense? Are they fair?
2. Can we allow students to break some rules but not others? Are there different types of rules?
3. How can we help these students with their problems? Is there any way that Alicia can pass a test without cheating? Can Kahlaa feel safe without having to carry a knife to school? Could Maria have found another way to follow the dress code and not break the rule? What would need to take place in the community to make these solutions possible?

2.3 Reflection

- What are some ideas or feelings you had in this lesson?
- What makes a rule fair?
- If there was a school rule you could change, what would it be and why?
- Are there rules that don't exist yet, but should?

CHAPTER 3
COURT POSITIONS

In Chapter 1, we learned that the goal of Youth Court is to help students take responsibility for their actions when they cause harm. Youth Courts start by helping them understand what the harm was, and then to think of ways to repair that harm.

How do we achieve that goal? Repairing harm is a very difficult task, but it's easier when we work as a group. Just like in a real courtroom, everyone in a Youth Court has a unique job to do. These jobs, or court positions, are equally important because they are all working towards a shared goal. See the next page for a list of Youth Court positions and their duties.

Glossary of Youth Court Positions

The **Judge** presides over the Youth Court to make sure everything is running smoothly, responsible for ensuring that everyone in the Youth Court is following directions and being respectful of each other and of the respondent.

The **Bailiff** sits next to the judge and helps him or her run the Youth Court, bringing the respondent and youth advocate in and out of the room and conducting the oaths at the beginning of the Court to swear in the respondent, youth advocate and jury.

The **Jury Foreperson** leads the jury during the questioning of the respondent, and calls on members of the jury to ask questions of the respondent. The jury foreperson is also responsible for filling out the paperwork once the jury has a disposition.

The **Sergeant-at-Arms** sits next to the jury foreperson and makes sure the questioning stays on track, counting the number of questions in each section and telling the jury foreperson when each section of the questioning is over to make sure the jury stays on track.

The **Clerk** is like a secretary for the Court, in charge of collecting the respondent's paperwork before the hearing, as well as explaining what the Court is and asking if the respondent would like to participate.

A **Jury** is a group of students who are present during the hearing to listen to the Youth Advocate's statements and decide on a resolution. When allowed by the judge, each Juror questions the respondent about the incident and encourages their peer to think about who they hurt and how they can change their behavior to avoid getting in trouble again. Jurors consider the factors that led to the harmful behavior, and must agree on a list of things the respondent has to do to make amends after the hearing (a disposition), and a date by which the actions on the list must be completed.

The **Youth Advocate** supports the respondent before, during and after the hearing to make sure the respondent's rights are being respected. The youth advocate prepares respondents before the hearing by letting them know what their rights are and what to expect on the day of the hearing. At the hearing, the youth advocate presents an opening statement that captures the respondent's side of the story, makes sure that the jury is asking appropriate questions, and later, makes a closing statement that summarizes the facts of the case.

A **Peer Mentor** (often the youth advocate) is assigned, only sometimes, by the jury to make sure that the disposition is followed through.

The **Respondent** is the student who has caused harm and has agreed to participate in the Youth Court. The respondent is supported by another student, the youth advocate, throughout the hearing process.

Activities

3.1 Brainstorm: What are court positions for?

For each court position, try to answer the following questions:

- What does this person / group do?
- How does the person in this position help achieve the goal of Youth Courts?
- What might be difficult about doing this job well?

3.2 Partial Mock Trial

In this mock trial, you will play the role of juror: Read the facts of this fictional case and discuss what action should take place. Remember, the role of a jury is to consider the factors that led to harmful behavior, and to come up with solutions that could prevent future harm from taking place.

> **Facts of the Case**
> A 20-year-old man is arrested and charged with theft from his employer. He lives with his younger sister and mother, who is disabled. She cannot work and gets by on a small disability check. The man graduated from community college. He lives at home, works at a local store, and gives his earnings to his mother as rent. He stole money from the cash register to buy his sister a prom dress. He has no record and the theft took place when nobody else was around—he paid back the amount taken.

Check-in: Do you understand the facts of the case? It's always okay to ask when you do not understand something.

3.3 Discuss:

- What is the jury's goal in their questioning? What kind of questions should they ask?
- What is the Youth Advocate's job? What should they say in their opening statement?
- Theft often results in jail time or probation. Is this fair? What would be a fair sentence in this situation? And why?

3.4 Reflection

- What are some ideas or feelings you had in this lesson?
- Which court positions would you be excited to try for yourself?
- Do you think a Youth Court needs these positions in order to repair harm? Why or why not?

CHAPTER 4
VALUES AND JUSTICE

In the previous chapter, we learned about the court positions and their responsibilities. However, these court positions can only be effective if they are guided by values, the core beliefs that we have, our principles or 'standards of behavior.' To put it another way, our values are the ways we judge what is important in life. They help us decide how to spend our time, our money and our energy. On an organizational level, values should guide the rules that a group of people agree to follow. Our rules and values help us to build strong relationships and live together peacefully.

When the rules of the organization in charge do not reflect the values of the people who answer to them, they have a right to speak up and demand change. Sometimes you may disagree with a school rule or someone else's actions or political views. In these cases, being able to identify and articulate your values will help you to speak up and advocate for yourself and others. Take an active role in discussing the conflict and remember that other people's values may be different from yours, but that does not make them wrong. Injustice occurs when a group of people are treated unfairly and forced into a system of laws that do not align with their own values and needs. Justice requires that everyone's needs and values are treated as equally important.

Activities

4.1 Brainstorm

1. What are your values? Do these values guide your decisions?
2. What do you think are your school's values? How do you see those values reflected in school?

4.2 Create a Value Board

1. Brainstorm a set of values that you, as a Youth Court, intend to uphold.

2. Why are these values important for a Youth Court?
3. If everyone agrees, write them on a large sheet of paper or poster board that will be displayed each time the group meets.

4.3 Brainstorm

1. Whose values and needs did the court prioritize?
2. What is equality? How do we establish it? Whose responsibility is it to ensure it?
3. What would you have said if you were Plessy's lawyer?

Sample of Values-Driven Court Case

Setting the Scene: After the Civil War, slavery was constitutionally abolished in 1865 with the 13th Amendment. In 1868, the 14th amendment was passed in an effort to establish racial equality under law.

The 14th Amendment: "No State shall make or enforce any law which shall abridge the privileges or immunities of citizens of the United States; nor shall any State deprive any person of life, liberty, or property, without due process of law; nor deny to any person within its jurisdiction the equal protection of the laws."

This legislation did not change the racist beliefs of former slave owners in the South, but it did help kick-start an era called Reconstruction, during which black Americans gained wealth and political power, created education campaigns and participated in boycotts of racist companies and organizations.

1896 - Plessy vs Ferguson: The Louisiana government had established the "Separate Car Act" which required that blacks and whites sit in separate railway cars. Homer Plessy, recruited by an activist group working to repeal the act, sat in and refused to vacate the whites-only car in 1892. He was arrested for violating the act. Although his lawyer argued that the Separate Car Act violated the 14th Amendment, the Louisiana Court overturned his case on the notion that the cars could be segregated by race as long as they were of similar quality. After losing twice in the lower courts, Plessy took his case to the U.S. Supreme Court, which upheld the previous decisions that racial segregation is constitutional under the separate but equal doctrine.

4.4 Brainstorm

1. Do you think our current legal system is just?
2. What are possible barriers delivering justice in court?

4.5 Reflection

1. What are some ideas or feelings you had in this lesson?
2. What shapes your values? Why are values important?
3. Are there things you value that your school also values? Are there things you value that your school doesn't value?
4. What does justice mean to you?

CHAPTER 5
DISCIPLINE AND PUNISHMENT

The purpose of discipline in schools is to teach students how to become responsible and caring adults. The original meaning of the word 'discipline' is to teach or to train. This includes helping students learn how to take responsibility for their actions, how to act with care and empathy, and how to communicate their needs effectively. Of course, this is what discipline should be. In reality, many schools use discipline as a method of controlling the student population. Especially in schools where tensions are high and/or resources are low, discipline means punishment.

Schools assign punishments to students for a few reasons. The main goal is to discourage students from future misbehavior by making them do something they normally wouldn't want to, like losing their free time to attend detention or missing school because of a suspension. Another goal is to "make an example" of student misbehavior by giving students the message: "If you do something bad to the school, the school will do something bad to you." In Youth Courts, we try to move away from this type of punitive discipline and towards a more restorative discipline. On the next page, you can find a chart outlining these differences.

Punitive Discipline	Restorative Discipline
An offense is a violation against the system, state, or school.	An offense is a harm done to people and the school community.
Justice requires the school administrators to determine blame (guilt) and impose pain (punishment).	Justice involves victims, offenders, and school-community members in an effort to repair the harm.

Punitive Discipline	Restorative Discipline
The offender passively accepts whatever punishment or consequences the school thinks he or she deserves.	The offender is encouraged to take responsibility for the harm that has been done and to help figure out what they need to do to rectify that harm.
The only thing preventing re-offense is punishment.	School helps the offender take active steps to prevent getting in trouble again.
Offenders are pushed out of school.	The offender is supported as a student and reintegrated into the school.
Accountability means accepting punishment.	Accountability means demonstrating empathy for the victim and a commitment to repairing the harm done.
The stigma of the offense stays with the offender. ("If a student breaks a rule, they're a bad student.")	The stigma of the offense is removable ("They're not a bad person, they just made a bad decision.")
"What rules have been broken? Who did it? What punishment do they deserve?"	"Who has been hurt? What are their needs? Who should fix what went wrong? How can we prevent this from happening again?"

Activities

5.1 Brainstorm: The Pros and Cons of Punishment

1. Do people get in trouble at your school? What are the punishments? What happens after a student gets suspended?
2. Why do schools punish students? Could there be a better way to discipline?
3. Do you think schools should get rid of punishment altogether? Why or why not?

5.2 Reflection

1. Does the sentence fit the crime? In other words, was a life sentence too much for the crime?
2. Does punishing someone help the person who gets in trouble? Do you think this experience would convince Shane to change his ways? Would it help him behave better?
3. Why do you think the lawmakers of California wanted to put people in jail for mild offenses? What would you do differently to help these people not get in trouble again?

Sample Case

Three-Strikes Laws and Shane Reams

Shane Reams stole from his neighbors' garages frequently, which upset his mother. She asked him to turn himself in after he was the lookout on a $20 drug sale. He already had two counts of burglary on his record. Because of California's three-strikes law, he received a life sentence because this was his third offense.

According to his mother, he lost hope because of the life sentence, so he joined a gang during his first several years in prison. When he learned that his mother was campaigning for his release, he began taking college courses within the prison and attending support groups. His mother successfully campaigned for his release and for legal reform to the three-strikes law, and Shane was finally released after 17 years of incarceration.

5.3 Advanced Reading: The School-to-Prison Pipeline

In the 1990s, schools across America began adopting "zero-tolerance policies"—strictly enforced bans against drugs, weapons and other misdemeanors that, if violated, lead to harsh punishments like suspension, expulsion or criminal sentencing. American lawmakers, eager to bring the "tough on crime" mantra of the War on Drugs into the classroom, passed the Gun-Free Schools Act of 1994, which required that states implement zero-tolerance policies for weapons violations or risk losing federal funding. Zero-tolerance policies have been criticized for being ineffective at actually lowering rates of crime or violence within schools, and for imposing on students an unfair and abusive approach to discipline.

Critics also point out that these increasingly harsh punishments and the widespread use of law enforcement in schools have been disproportionately used against students of color. Black students are suspended and expelled 3.5 times more than white students are, and represent 31% of school-related arrests (despite making up less than 13% of the country's student population). Black girls are 10 times more likely to receive discipline referrals than white girls. This system of control has been called the "school-to-prison pipeline," because the criminalization of students consequently pushes them into the criminal-justice system.

When students get suspended or expelled, they are statistically more likely to enter the criminal-justice system later in life. Students who do not graduate from high school are eight times more likely to end up in jail or prison. Black and Latino students, as well as students with disabilities, are especially vulnerable to the school-to-prison pipeline because they are subject to disproportionate scrutiny and punishment.

The United States incarcerates more of its citizens than any other country in the world, with 2.3 million people in jail or prison today; this is what we mean when talking about mass incarceration in America. The school-to-prison pipeline is one piece of this much larger machine, and it is important that we consider both when we talk about racism in America. Mass incarceration and the school-to-prison pipeline are examples of institutional racism: harm that is done to nonwhite people through a political system of power and control.

5.4 Reflection

- What are some ideas or feelings you had in this lesson?
- Why do schools punish students? What are the consequences of punishment? Could there be a better way to discipline?
- Were you previously familiar with the issue of mass incarceration before? How does it feel to learn about America's history of racism?

CHAPTER 6
RESTORATIVE JUSTICE

In Chapter 5, we learned about the differences between punitive and restorative discipline. This idea of doing things restoratively comes from the model of restorative justice—using a collaborative process to understand the harm and work together to repair it. Sounds a lot like Youth Courts, right? If you've made it this far in the handbook, you get the idea by now: Crime and rule-breaking causes harm, and that harm creates an obligation for the harmer to "put things right." If restorative justice was a wheel, there would be four spokes holding it together: (1) focusing on harm and needs; (2) addressing the obligations that the harm created; (3) involving stakeholders (anyone who has an interest in seeing the harm rectified): people who were harmed, people who caused the harm, and their communities; and (4) using a collaborative process (such as Youth Courts) to make a plan of action. This would be the wheel of "putting things right." Respect would be the road it travels because restorative justice can only function if it is grounded in respect for everyone involved.

Asking Questions for Restorative Justice

If you are part of the jury, you are in a position to make sure that the disposition will be helpful and restorative. In order to do this, you must understand the respondent's situation well enough to create a disposition that helps them to repair and strengthen their relationship with themselves and others.

Ask questions that provide you with a thorough understanding of the incident that took place: What happened? What is the harm? What happened before and after? How does each party feel? What relationships are involved? What are the dynamics of these relationships?

Kinds of Questions:

Fact questions: Understand the where, when, what and who of the situation.

Harm questions: Understand the harm (or harms) caused.

Fix-it questions: Understand how the respondent envisions repairing the harm caused.

Good Questioning: Use Compassion

- You can ask more direct questions than you think you can;
- You can care about the people and situation at hand; and
- You can offer encouragement or advice you may have gained from personal experience.

Activities

6.1 Brainstorm

- How do Youth Courts follow the principles of restorative justice described above? How do they not? If you identify differences, why do you think this is?

- How would you define harm, needs and obligations?
- What would make it difficult to do a restorative-discipline process at your school?

6.2 Practice

One person should take on the role of the respondent, and everyone else is part of the jury (see pages 8-9 for court positions). Together, the jury will ask the respondent questions starting in order of fact, harm and then fix-it questions to build an understanding of the respondent's actions and situation. The respondent will use the school referral and student statement below to build his or her backstory, and the jury will use the phases of questions to guide the inquiry process. Then the jury will then create a disposition that is thorough and restorative. Feel free to divide into two different juries, each working with a different respondent so that everyone participates. If you do this, make sure to discuss your experiences together afterwards!

6.3 Reflection

- What are some ideas or feelings you had in this lesson?
- What did you notice about the questioning process? What was it like to be part of the jury? To be the respondent?
- What do you think is the most challenging part of a restorative process?
- What questions do you have about what we've learned so far?

CHAPTER 7
CONFLICT RESOLUTION

Have you had a disagreement with someone that you didn't know how to resolve? Have you ever felt upset or angry with another person enough to do something hurtful? These are examples of conflicts. A conflict is a disagreement or fight between two or more people, and having or witnessing one can be difficult. Conflicts can bring up strong negative emotions in us: anger, embarrassment, fear and helplessness, to name a few. These powerful emotions have been the driving forces behind conflicts between groups of people throughout history. If conflicts are driven by emotions, then the key to resolving these conflicts is understanding our own emotions and how they shape our needs and desires. If we can do this for ourselves, we can negotiate with the people around us to find a way to resolve conflicts with compassion and care.

At school, you've probably seen how conflicts can arise between students, between students and teachers, and even between adults. When we don't take the time to understand a conflict and, instead, let it make us angry, we can cause harm. Oftentimes, conflict arises because of some previous harm, so reacting this way can feel like the right thing to do. However, trading harm for harm will only continue a cycle of conflict, not end it. Conflict resolution is the process of finding a solution to the conflict through communication. When we handle it well, conflict can help us understand ourselves and each other better. With conflict-resolution skills, we can build stronger relationships and a more peaceful community.

Key

It is important to identify things that trigger strong emotions for you. When you know what they are, you can anticipate the feelings that will come when you encounter them, and be better prepared to address each while acknowledging the feeling: "Yes, I am angry" and you can control how you react to it: "No, I will not let my anger cause harm to others or myself!" This is difficult to do, but as you practice, you can strengthen your capacity for self-awareness and self-control just like you can strengthen a muscle.

Keys to Resolving Conflict

- Commitment: Believe in each other and in the conflict-resolution process. If everyone is committed and willing, resolving a conflict can be a beneficial and empowering process for everyone.
- Manage emotion: Anger, stress, panic or other strong feelings can make it difficult to think clearly, to listen well to other people, and to express your own thoughts and feelings. It is important to let these feelings roll off before engaging in a conflict-resolution process.
- Listen and empathize: Stay curious, listen closely to what others say so that you understand each person's side of the story, and their feelings and needs. Ask questions to clarify as needed!
    - "How did this event affect you?"
    - "What are you feeling?"
    - "Are there other events that are contributing to how you feel about this specific incident?"
- Identify the cause of the conflict: Conflict is often caused by miscommunication and is the symptom of more than just one incident.
- Accountability: If someone has harmed or hurt the feelings of someone else it is important that they understand and take responsibility for their actions.
- Negotiate: Perhaps talking through the conflict has resolved it, or something else is still needed like an apology or commitment for future interactions. Develop an action plan together and move forward with a better understanding of each other.

Activities

7.1 Know Your Triggers

- Write down 8-10 things that annoy or anger you. What do you feel when people do these things? How do you react?
- Share 2-3 of the points you wrote down.
- Are the reactions that you tend to have similar or different from each other? In what ways?

7.2 Practice

> **Sample Issue**
> **School Referral:** "Mr. Jordan reports that Jamar yelled and cursed at Keyanna for not wanting to be his project partner."
>
> **Student Statement:** "I was really angry that she doesn't want to be my partner, so I just shouted at her."
>
> One of Jamar's teachers interrupted him and did not let him finish his sentence. That made him feel upset and unimportant. After that, Jamar tripped in the hallway and felt embarrassed. Keyanna not wanting to be Jamal's partner was the third upsetting thing that had happened to him that day. Had it been the only thing that happened, he probably would not have reacted so negatively.

- What questions would you ask Jamar to better understand how he reacted?
- What is the source (or sources) of conflict in this scenario? What made Jamar angry?
- What else could Jamar have done? Use your behavior-chain analysis!
- What could Jamar have done better?
- What could be helpful for Jamar to hear?

7.3 Reflection

- What are some ideas or feelings you had in this lesson?

- Think of a conflict you have experienced or witnessed:
- Can you identify the cause (or multiple causes) of the conflict?
- What were you feeling at the time?
- Would you change how you acted during the conflict? If so, why and how would you act differently?
- What strengths can you bring to resolving conflicts? What skills do you want more practice with?

CHAPTER 8
HOW TO RUN A YOUTH COURT

Over the course of this handbook, we've learned about justice, values, rules and fairness. With this knowledge, we're ready to practice a new skill: running a full Youth Court session!

Jury Questioning

In Youth Courts, the jury asks three types of questions: **fact, harm, and fix-it**. Jury questioning is usually divided into these three separate phases:

1. **Fact** questions establish the facts of the case and usually begin with "Who?" "What?" "When?" "Where?" "Why?" or "How?" For example: "What was happening before this event took place?" or "How did you feel when that happened?"
2. **Harm** questions encourage the respondent to reflect on who was affected by their actions and what harm occurred. For example: "How do you think your actions have affected this person?" or "Do you believe you've caused harm? Why or why not?"
3. **Fix-it** questions encourage the respondent to figure out how to repair the harm and make things right. For example: "What do you think needs to happen to make this situation right?" or "Do you wish to apologize to the person for what you did? What would you say?"

Read the following hypothetical case referral, and try to think of the fact, harm, and fix-it questions you would need answers to in order to make a disposition.

School Referral: "Jamilah was referred to Youth Court for swearing at a teacher during class last week. The teacher had asked Jamilah to leave the classroom, and they were arguing when Jamilah swore at her and walked out."

YOUTH COURT PROCESS AND SCRIPT

Full Mock Trial

In this mock trial, every court position will be filled by somebody, including someone to play the fictional respondent. Refer back to Chapter 3 for a refresher on the court positions. A script is provided below to help guide you through the process. As youth advocate, your job for this mock trial will be to work with your respondent to have a story straight, so that you can answer the jury's questions. You can use the above school referral or this one:

> **School Referral:** "Over the weekend, Kevin and five other students snuck into the school and spray-painted graffiti on several lockers. Footage from outside surveillance cameras identified all students involved. Kevin was cooperative and admitted to being involved in the incident."

> **Student Statement:** "I know what I did was wrong and I'm sorry. I was hanging out with my friends and we were bored. When one of them said we should try sneaking into the school, a few of us didn't want to at first, but then we did anyway—I guess it was peer pressure. I hope I can fix it without getting kicked out of school or something."

Opening of Youth Court

JUDGE: The court will come to order. Bailiff, please bring the respondent and youth advocate into the court.

Bailiff brings the respondent and youth advocate into the room.

JUDGE: Respondent and youth advocate, please remain standing.

BAILIFF: All rise. Youth Court is starting. ____________________ (Name of judge) is judging case number __________ (fill in the blank), the case of ______________________ (name of respondent.) Everyone please stand up.

1. Please raise your right hand and repeat after me:
   I swear that everything I see or hear in Youth Court today will be kept a secret. Everyone please sit except for the jury.

2. Please raise your right hand:
   Do you promise that you will be fair when looking at the evidence today and that you will come to a disposition according to the Youth Court rules? (Everyone should say yes.) Please sit down.
3. Respondent and youth advocate, please stand and raise your right hand. Do you promise that you are going to tell the truth, the whole truth, and nothing but the truth? (They should say yes.) Please sit down.

JUDGE: In Youth Court we need the same level of respect that people show in any courtroom. Please pay attention to these rules:

- Do not chew gum, eat, or drink.
- Do not use cell phones or other electronics.
- Laughing or talking when it is not your turn is not allowed.
- If people are not following the rules, the bailiff or I will ask that you stop.
- If we are ignored, whoever is breaking the rules will have to leave the room and the hearing will continue without them.
- If the respondent is not following the rules, they will have to leave, and we won't be able to finish the trial.

Does everyone understand? (Everyone says yes). Bailiff, please read the statements from the school and the respondent.

BAILIFF: (Reads statements.)

JUDGE: Youth advocate, please make your opening statement.

YOUTH ADVOCATE: Makes opening statement.

JUDGE: Respondent, do you want to say anything before the jury starts to ask questions?

RESPONDENT: Responds yes or no.

JUDGE: The jury can now ask the respondent questions.

JURY FOREPERSON: Calls on jurors to ask questions in the order that they raise their hands. (*Fact* questions are asked first followed by *harm* questions and finally, *fix-it* questions).

JURY FOREPERSON: When all the *fact* questions have been asked, the jury foreperson says: We can move onto questions about *harm*.

JURY FOREPERSON: When all *harm* questions have been asked the jury foreperson asks: Do any jurors have any more *harm* questions?

JURY FOREPERSON: When all *fix-it* questions have been asked the jury foreperson asks: Do any jurors have any more *fix-it* questions?

CLOSING STATEMENT, JURY DISCUSSION, AND DISPOSITION

JUDGE: Youth advocate, please make your closing statement.

YOUTH ADVOCATE makes closing statement.

JUDGE: Bailiff, please take the respondent and youth advocate out of the room.

The respondent and youth advocate leave, and the bailiff comes back.

JUDGE: The jury may now begin its discussion.

The jury talks until they reach a decision, and the jury foreperson writes it down.

JURY FOREPERSON: Your honor, we have made a decision.

JUDGE: Bailiff, please bring the respondent and youth advocate back into the room.

BAILIFF: Respondent and youth advocate, please stay standing.

JUDGE: Jury, please stand up. Jury foreperson, please read your decision to the court and the respondent.

JURY FOREPERSON: We, the members of the ________________ (say the name of your school) Youth Court have made this decision: (Read the decision to the court).

JUDGE: ______________ (respondent's name), do you understand the decision? (Wait for them to say yes or no.) Are you going to complete it? (Wait for them to say yes or no.) Do you understand that if you do not complete it, your case will go back to your school for further action? (Wait for them to say yes or no.)

JUDGE: Court is now over (taps gavel). Bailiff, please take the respondent and youth advocate back outside to complete the decision contract.

The respondent and youth advocate leave with the bailiff to sign the contract.

8.1 Reflection

- What are some ideas or feelings you had in this lesson?
- Did anything surprise or annoy you during the court proceeding?
- Now that you're ready to run entire Youth Court sessions, are there other skills or topics you'd like to learn about?

INDEX
OF GROUP ACTIVITIES

Below you can find some games and activities that are fun for students and help reinforce the collaborative group work necessary for Youth Courts. These can also be applied to the reflection and brainstorming activities that appear in each chapter.

Activities for Discussion, Reflection and Brainstorming Sections

1. Pair and Share

- Turn to the person next to you and discuss the questions with one another.
- Share with the rest of the group what you talked about.

2. Pop-Corn

- Each person offers their thoughts and reflections in no particular order.
- Students take turns speaking without calling on each other; this requires patience and active listening so as not to talk over one another.

3. Pass the Torch

- The teacher calls on someone to share.
- After sharing, this person will choose someone else to share and so on.
- This activity can be done so that each person is sharing based on the same question, or you can have each person prompt the next person with a different question.

4. Free Write

Each person takes 1-5 minutes to reflect on their thoughts or feelings. Different free-write prompts include:

- Check for understanding: Write down any questions you have.

- Flow of consciousness: Write whatever comes to your mind.
- Write a summary of what you have learned.

5. Spectrum

- Designate one side of the classroom as the "agree" side and the other as "disagree."
- The facilitator or teacher will say a series of statements about the topic the students just explored.
- For each topic, students will stand on the "agree" side if they agree, the "disagree" side if they don't and somewhere in the middle if they are undecided or attached to both.
- After each student has decided on their place, the facilitator will call on students from every side to explain where they stand and why.

Sample Statements:

- *"Restorative justice can be healing to everyone involved."*
- *"Rules exist to control you."*
- *"Some teachers are out to get students."*
- *"It is more important for the youth advocate to make the jury pity the respondent."*
- *"Conflict-resolution skills only work in certain situations."*

Team-Building and Fun Activities

1. **Strength** - Divide into teams of 4-6 people, with each having a large piece of paper and some markers. Each person on the team should list out strengths they have, write these on the piece of paper and draw these attributes into a person, a character that now needs a name! Then, create a small story about how this person would resolve a conflict and share with the rest of the class (either telling, acting out or drawing the story).
2. **Construction** - Pair up with another person, each pair receiving a piece of computer paper. Each pair should work together to build the highest stable structure using nothing other than that piece of paper. When time is up, discuss what worked and what didn't—both in structures and in communication with one another.

3. **Birthday** - Everyone must line up in order of their birthday from youngest to oldest (to the day) without saying a word to each other. To make this one more challenging, add a 2-minute timer.

4. **Step Across the Line** - Everyone stands in two lines facing each other about 4 feet apart. The facilitator will say a series of "I" statements, and if this statement is true for you, step forward onto the imaginary line between the two groups. This activity is intended to help everyone get to know each other as well as become aware of the vast variety of experiences that each group member brings to the table and that, together, everyone shares. Depending on the statements used, this exercise can bring up difficult memories and requires trust and vulnerability.

5. **The Human Knot** - For this one you will need a space big enough that everyone can stand in a circle! So... stand in a circle, close your eyes, reach your hands to the center of the circle and grasp any two hands you can find with your eyes closed. Open your eyes! Everyone should be holding the hands of 1 or 2 other people in the circle; your task now is to, without letting go of anyone's hands, untie the knot that has been created so that you are all standing in a circle and the people whose hands you are holding stand next to you. This one is difficult but satisfying! For an extra challenge, do it without speaking out loud.

GLOSSARY OF TERMS

Confidential - Information that must be kept secret within a specific group of people.

Conflict - An active disagreement or fight between people, usually over opposing opinions or needs.

Consensus - Reaching an agreement between multiple people.

Disproportionate - Too big or too small in comparison to something else.

Escalation - The process of a conflict growing in intensity because of heightened emotions or irrational behavior.

Harm - The negative impact that our actions and words can have on ourselves and the people around us, and the negative effects that directly result from the respondent's action(s).

Imposed - Forced to be accepted or put into place.

Needs - The physical or psychological requirements for a person's well-being.

Obligation - Something to which a person is morally or legally bound—a person's duty or commitment.

Punitive Justice - The belief that justice requires that misbehavior or violation of the law be met with retribution or punishment—a form of justice that relies on rules to define consequences for causing harm.

Provocation - An act that intends to make someone angry or upset.

Restorative Justice - A form of justice that prioritizes people over rules. Restorative justice requires a collaborative process of understanding harm, establishing accountability, and repairing harm and personal relationships.

School Referral - Brief statement written by a teacher or principal describing their perspective of the student respondent's behavior.

Student Statement - Brief statement written by the student respondent describing the what and the why of their behavior.

Made in the USA
Monee, IL
23 June 2026

55592734R00024